YEARS 3 & 4

MULTIPLICATION & DIVISION

Do you need to know the basics of multiplication and division? Let's learn about them together.

Parents and carers are encouraged to read the explanation and practice sections with their child.

Ann Baker

Illustrated by Janice Bowles

About this book

Each unit in this book begins with a brief **explanation** of a concept or a strategy. You are encouraged to read this explanation with your child and, where appropriate, to use everyday materials and examples to give meaning to the concepts.

We practise is a worked example for you and your child to discuss together, paying particular attention to the thinking processes required to understand the concept or apply the strategy.

You practise gives your child the opportunity to practise the concept or strategy. It also indicates how well your child understands the new material and often includes problem-solving questions to ensure that your child has mastered the concept or strategy.

If further support is required, you and your child's teacher can devise a plan to ensure that all the basic concepts are fully understood and consolidated.

The **Tests** at the end of the book are provided to check that the concepts are fully understood. Test 1 can be done after units 1–10 are completed and Test 2 when the book is finished.

Meet 'BOB' – Back Of the Book

At the end of each unit, BOB reminds your child to go to the Answers section at the back of the book.

Mathematical Content

This book has been designed to cover the concepts of multiplication and division that your child will encounter in **Year 3** and **Year 4**. The units provide a comprehensive coverage of the following Key Topics from the **Australian Curriculum: Mathematics.**

Australian Curriculum : Mathematics

YEAR 3

Recall multiplication facts of two, three, five and ten and related division facts (ACMNA056)

Represent and solve problems involving multiplication using efficient mental and written strategies and appropriate digital technologies (ACMNA057)

YEAR 4

Recall multiplication facts up to 10 × 10 and related division facts (ACMNA075)

Develop efficient mental and written strategies and use appropriate digital technologies for multiplication and for division where there is no remainder (ACMNA076)

Contents & Checklist

WRITING and TALKING ABOUT MULTIPLICATION and DIVISION

Multiplication

The multiplication sign is ×.

Multiplication is the quick way to do repeated addition.

$\underbrace{4 + 4 + 4 + 4 + 4}_{\text{five 4s}} = 20 \qquad 5 \times 4 = 20$

There are many words that mean multiply.

For example **5 × 4** can also be said as:

5 times 4
5 multiplied by 4
5 lots of 4
5 equal-sized groups of 4.

The result of a multiplication is often called the **product**.
For example, in 5 × 4 = 20,
20 is the **product of 5 and 4.**

Division

The division sign is ÷.

Division is the quick way to do repeated subtraction.

$20 - \underbrace{4 + 4 + 4 + 4 + 4}_{\text{five 4s}} = 0 \qquad 20 \div 4 = 5$

There are many words that mean divide.

For example **20 ÷ 4 = 5** can be said as:

20 divided by 4 equals 5
20 shared into 5 groups of 4
4 goes into 20 five times.

The result of a division is sometimes called the **quotient**.
For example, in 20 ÷ 4 = 5,
5 is the **quotient of 20 and 4.**

Fact family

Multiplication and division are related in the same way as addition and subtraction.

3 × 4 = 12   4 × 3 = 12

12 ÷ 3 = 4   12 ÷ 4 = 3

All of these four facts are part of **one multiplication fact family** and you will often find that knowing a multiplication fact can help you find the answer to a division question.

When multiplying, it doesn't matter if you swap the numbers around. 4 × 5 is the same as 5 × 4.

GAME CARD IDEAS

Cut out the game cards – they will last longer if they are laminated. Here are some games for you to try.

Highest or lowest PRODUCT

A game for two players.

Use the **multiplication** cards for this game.

Each player is dealt three cards. At the beginning of each round, a coin is flipped. 'Heads' means the highest product wins and 'tails' means the lowest product wins. Players select their best card and lay it on the table. The player with the winning total wins that pair of cards. Then each player takes a new card, ready for the next round. The player with the most pairs when the cards run out is the winner.

There is some strategy to this game. It is not always a good idea to play your lowest card when 'tails' is flipped. If your lowest card is the least possible, you might want to save it for later so that you are certain of winning a point.

Matching fact pairs

A game for two players.

Dealt four cards to each player from both sets of cards. On their turn, a player looks for a pair of cards from the same multiplication fact family, such as 6 × 7 and 42 ÷ 7, then lays them down in their own pile and replaces them with two cards ready for the next round. If a player cannot make a pair, they discard one card into the discard pile and replace it from the pack. When the pack runs out, shuffle the discard pile and use it as a new pack.

The player with the most pairs when the cards run out is the winner.

Highest or lowest QUOTIENT

A game for two players.

This game is played as above, but with the **division** cards.

NOTE: Games are meant to be fun and provide practice without stress. It is recommended that in the early stages you play with the cards visible on the table to allow for discussion and hints, and that you stop playing while you are still having fun and then your child will want to play again another time.

USING DOUBLES for MULTIPLICATION

When you buy things in a packet, there are ways to work out how many items are in the packet.

For example, eggs come in a carton of 12.

You can see that there are either **2 rows of 6** or **6 rows of 2**. Whichever way you multiply the rows, the answer is the same, **2 × 6 = 12** or **6 × 2 = 12**.

How can you work out how many muffins are in this packet?

You can use **doubles** to find the answer.

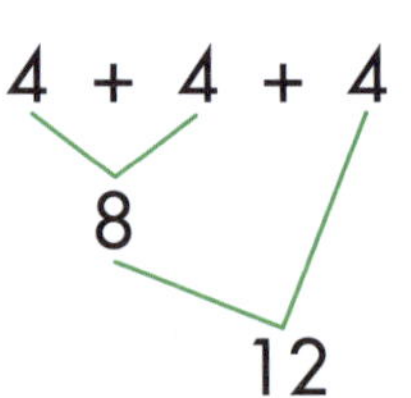

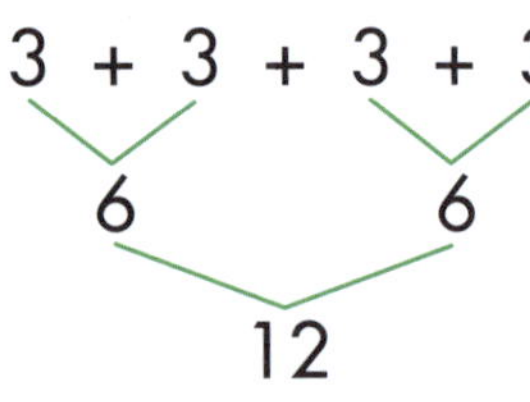

Either way, the answer is 12.

We practise

Write two multiplication sentences to show how many biscuits are in this packet.

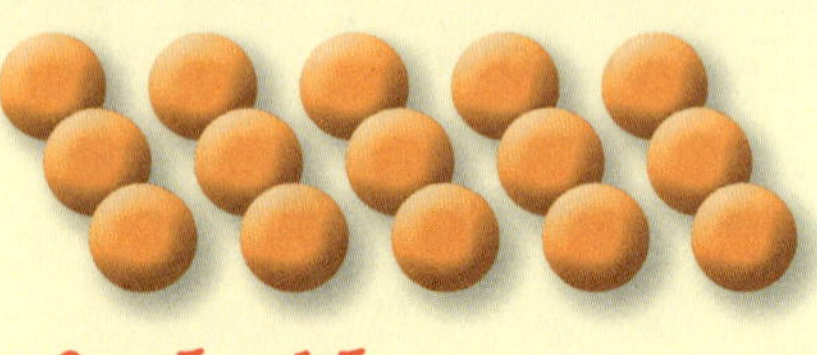

3 × 5 = 15
5 × 3 = 15

Show how doubles can be used to find the answer to this addition.

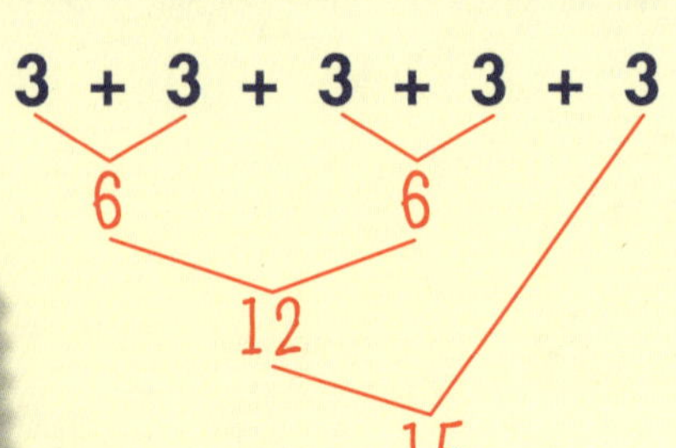

You practise

Write two multiplication sentences that show how many biscuits are in each packet.

____ × ____ = ____

____ × ____ = ____

____ × ____ = ____

____ × ____ = ____

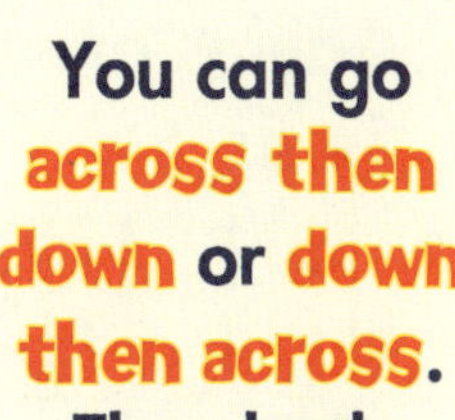

____ × ____ = ____

____ × ____ = ____

____ × ____ = ____

____ × ____ = ____

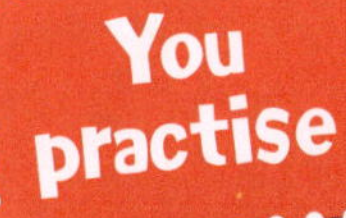

Work out the answer to each question using doubles. Write the matching multiplication sentence.

4 + 4 + 4 + 4 = ____ ____ × ____ = ____

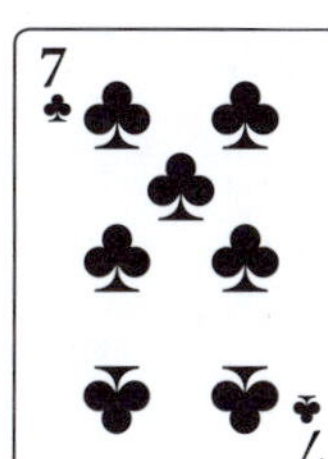
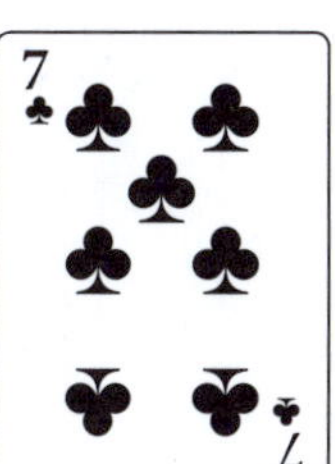

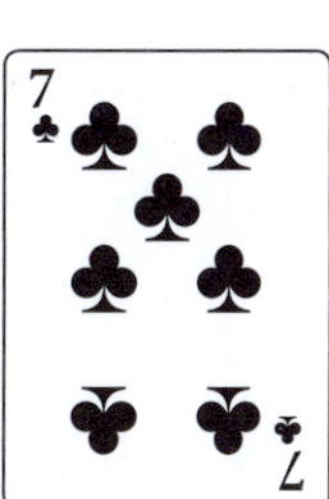

7 + 7 + 7 + 7 + 7 = ____ ____ × ____ = ____

BOB time!

TALLIES

Tallies are easy to **skip count** because they come in 5s.

5 10 15 20 25 30

6 × 5 = 30

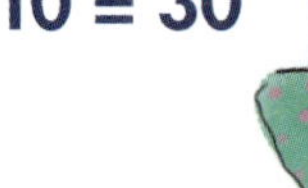

Tallies are even easier to skip count in **10s**.

10 20 30

3 × 10 = 30

Tallies can help with learning multiplication tables and with problem solving. Look at this example.

How many legs on six ants?

6 × 5 = 30
6 × 1 = 6
36

Answer: There are 36 legs on 6 ants.

These tallies show **6 × 5**.

We practise

Use tallies to work out how many days in 3 weeks.

3 × 5 = 15
3 × 2 = 6
21

There are 21 days in 3 weeks.

Use tallies to show 4 × 12.

4 × 5 = 20
4 × 5 = 20
4 × 2 = 8
48

4 × 12 = 48

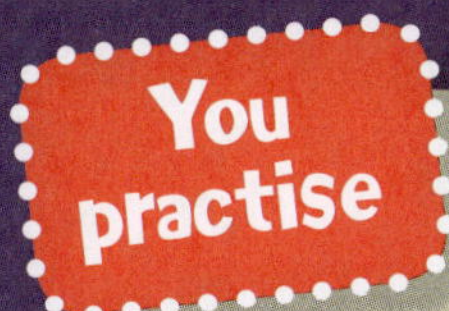

Use tallies to work out each of the following.

How many legs on 4 spiders?

There are _____ legs on 4 spiders.

How many days in 5 weeks?

There are _____ days in 5 weeks.

How many dots on these dice?

 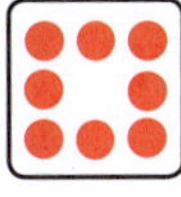 

There are _____ dots on the dice.

How many legs on these ants?

There are _____ legs on 5 ants.

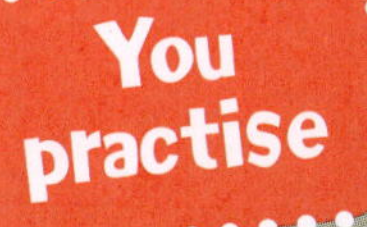

Use tallies to show each multiplication.

$3 \times 8 =$ _____

$5 \times 8 =$ _____

$3 \times 13 =$ _____

8 $4 \times 15 =$ _____

BOB time!

FOUR WAYS TO SOLVE A PROBLEM

This poster shows the same multiplication problem in four ways: in **words**, as a **picture**, as a **repeated addition** and as a **multiplication**.

Words	Picture
Jake threw four 4s with his dice. What was his score? You need to spot that the problem is a multiplication question.	  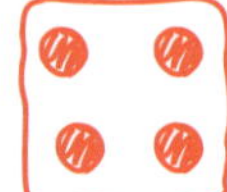  You could draw a picture of the problem to help you work out the answer.
Repeated addition	**Multiplication**
4 + 4 + 4 + 4 You could use addition and doubles to find the answer to the problem.	**4 × 4 = 16** Actually writing the multiplication sentence is the best way to solve this problem (if you remember your 4 times tables).

It is always a good idea to solve a problem in more than one way. Then you can be sure that your answer is correct.

We practise

Draw a picture for this word problem.

There are 5 ants in an ant farm. How many legs do they have altogether?

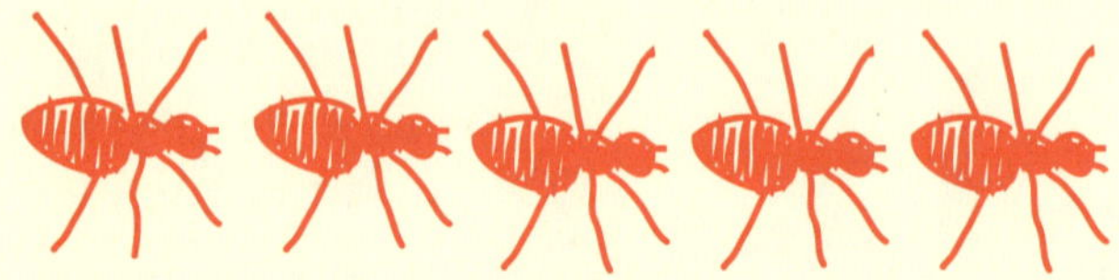

They have 30 legs altogether.

Write the multiplication sentence for the problem.

How many petals on these flowers?

4 × 5 = 20

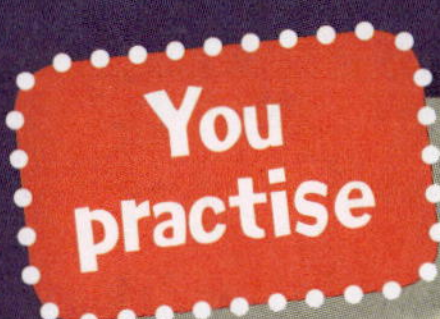

Draw a picture to work out the answer to each problem.

There are 5 boxes of balls.
Each box contains 4 balls.
How many balls altogether?

____ × ____ = ______

There are 3 bags of lollies
with 6 lollies in each bag.
How many lollies altogether?

____ × ____ = ______

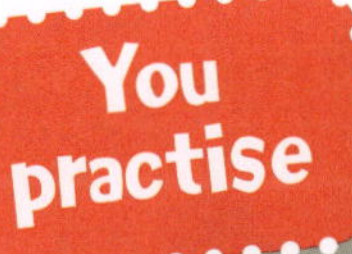

Write the multiplication sentence for each picture.

How many legs on the spiders?

____ × ____ = ______

How many tallies?

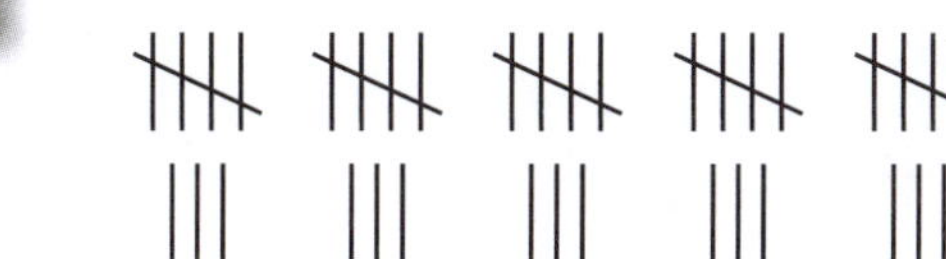

____ × ____ = ______

Complete this Four Ways poster.

Words The shopkeeper sold Jake 4 bags of marbles, with 11 marbles in each bag. How many marbles are there altogether?	**Picture**
Repeated addition ____ + ____ + ____ + ____	**Multiplication** ____ × ____ = ____

BOB time!

UNIT 4

EQUAL-SIZED JUMPS

To win one of the prizes in this spinning wheel game at the fair, you have to make more than one equal-sized jump from 'Start' to land on the toy that you want.

For example, to win the wind-up mouse on number 9, you would need to make three jumps of 3.

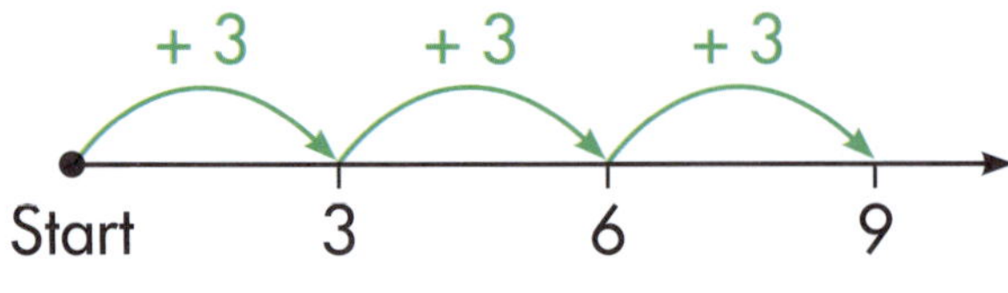

3 jumps of 3 or **3 × 3 = 9** to win the mouse.

We practise

Show the equal-sized jumps needed to win the wind-up bear.

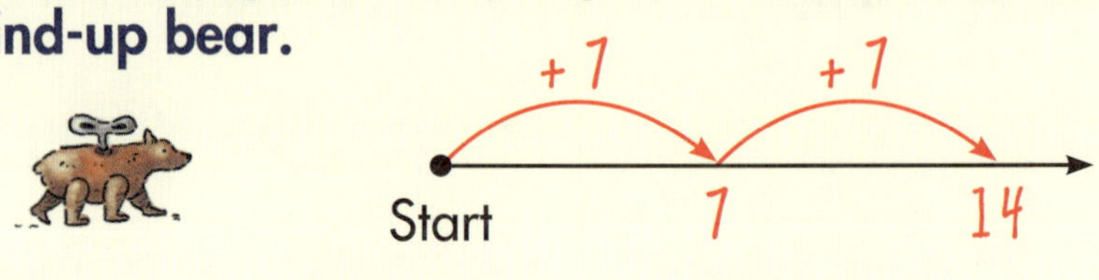

You practise Use the spinning wheel on the opposite page to answer each question.

1. Show how you can get to the lollies in jumps of 2. 

Start ______ × ______ = ______

2. Show how you can get to the rocking horse in jumps of 4. 

Start

______ × ______ = ______

3. On your first jump you get to the bucket and spade. How many more jumps to get to the teddy bear?  

Start ______ more jumps

4. In jumps of 5, what is the closest you can get to the babushka doll? 

______ × ______ = ______

5. In three jumps you got to the pool duck. What size were your jumps? 

______

7. You can only make two jumps to get to the ball. What number do you land on first? 

______

6. You only want to make three jumps to get to the telephone. What size jumps should you make?

______ 

8. If your first jump is to the skipping rope, how many jumps do you have to make to get to the red truck?

______

BOB time!

MULTIPLICATION TURNAROUNDS

Jake and Clare each have 12 cherries on a plate.
They both like to arrange their cherries in a special way before eating them.

Jake has 3 lots of 4 cherries.
3 × 4 = 12

Clare has 4 lots of 3 cherries.
4 × 3 = 12

3 × 4 and **4 × 3** are related multiplication sentences, called **turnarounds**.

You know about turnarounds for addition:
3 + 4 = 7 and 4 + 3 = 7
It's the same for multiplication:
3 × 4 = 12 and 4 × 3 = 12

These five dice are each showing 2.

There are **five lots of 2**.
5 × 2 = 10

These two dice are each showing 5.

There are **two lots of 5**.
2 × 5 = 10

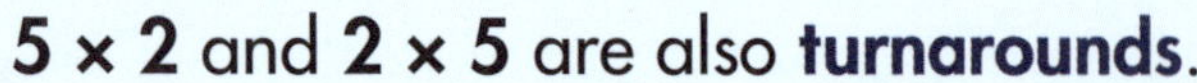

5 × 2 and **2 × 5** are also **turnarounds**.

We practise

Write the turnaround for the multiplication sentence.

3 × 6 = 18
6 × 3 = 18

Write two related multiplication sentences for the number 21.

7 × 3 = 21
3 × 7 = 21

You practise Write the turnaround for each multiplication sentence.

 4 × 6 = 24 ____ × ____ = ______

 5 × 4 = 20 ____ × ____ = ______

 5 × 6 = 30 ____ × ____ = ______

 4 × 8 = 32 ____ × ____ = ______

Just think of the **turnaround.** That makes it easy.

You practise Write two related multiplication sentences for each number.

 **35** 7 × ____ = ______ ____ × ____ = ______

 **36** 4 × ____ = ______ ____ × ____ = ______

 **24** 4 × ____ = ______ ____ × ____ = ______

 **60** 6 × ____ = ______ ____ × ____ = ______

 **27** ____ × ____ = ______ ____ × ____ = ______

 **28** ____ × ____ = ______ ____ × ____ = ______

BOB time!

UNIT 6

MORE THAN – LESS THAN

Jake and Clare are playing More Than – Less Than, a game that uses two piles of cards.

4 sets of cards in this pile, numbers 1 to 5

2 sets of cards in this pile, numbers 1 to 9

On her turn, Clare takes two cards – one from each pile. Her job is to make a close estimate of the product of the two cards.

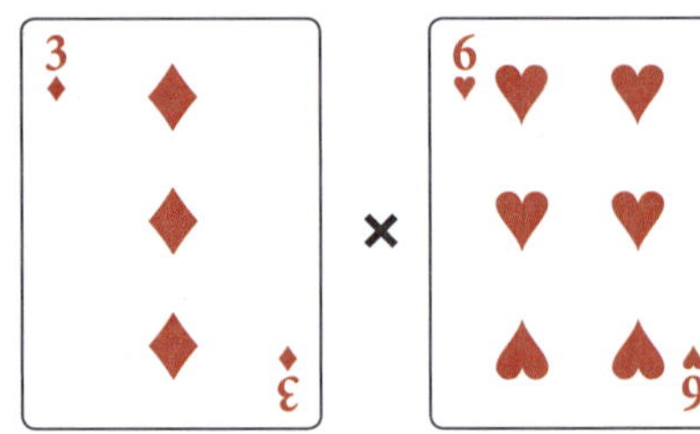

Her estimate has to be a **multiple of 5** and because she knows that **3 × 5 = 15**, she calls **'more than 15'**.

Jake checks her multiplication with this key sequence on the calculator: **3 × 6 = 18**

Clare wins a point because the answer is more than 15, but less than 20 (which is the next multiple of 5).

These are Jake's two cards. He calls **'less than 20'** because he knows his doubles.

Clare checks his multiplication with this key sequence on the calculator: **2 × 8 = 16**

So Jake also wins a point because 16 is less than 20, but more than 15.

We practise

Write your estimate for the product of these two cards and the reason why you chose that estimate. Then check on your calculator.

Estimate	Reason	Check	Win/Lose
More than 20	4 x 5 = 20	4 x 6 = 24	Win

You practise Write your estimate and reason for each pair of cards.

1 3 × 

Estimate	Reason	Check	Win/Lose

2 4 × 

Estimate	Reason	Check	Win/Lose

You practise Both piles now contain cards 6–9.
Write your estimate and reason for each pair of cards.

  × 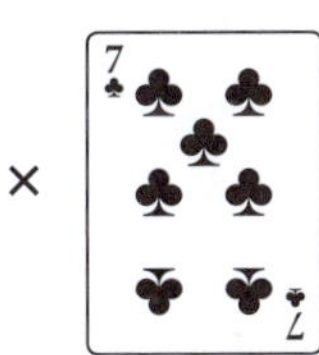

Estimate	Reason	Check	Win/Lose

 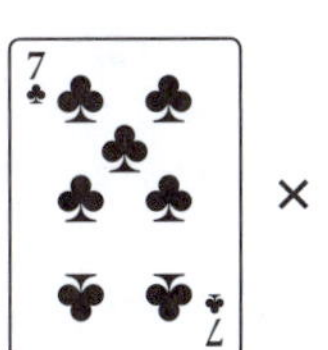 × 

Estimate	Reason	Check	Win/Lose

  × 

Estimate	Reason	Check	Win/Lose

 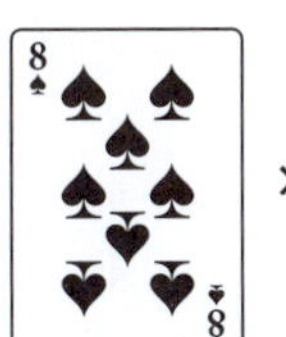 × 

Estimate	Reason	Check	Win/Lose

  × 

Estimate	Reason	Check	Win/Lose

  × 

Estimate	Reason	Check	Win/Lose

BOB time!

CLOSEST to 50

Jake and Clare often play Closest to 50 with a pack of cards that uses only the numbers 1–10.

In the game, each player takes three cards from the top of the pile and chooses two of these cards to multiply together.

The person whose product is closest to 50 wins a point.

A calculator is used to check that the right person has scored the point.

These are Jake's cards.

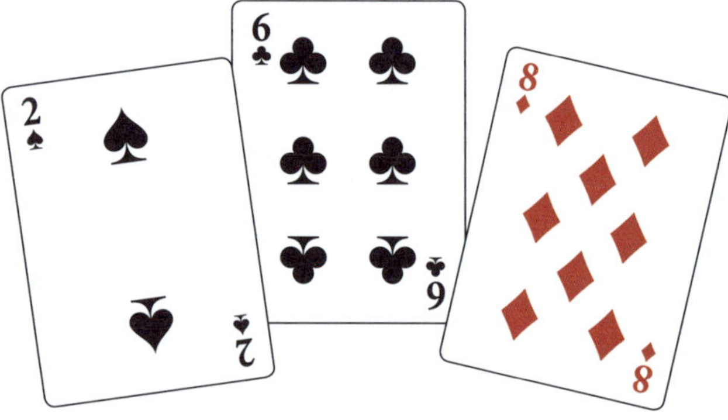

Jake chooses the 6 and the 8 and uses this key sequence on the calculator to find out how close he is to 50:

50 − 6 × 8 = 2

These are Clare's cards.

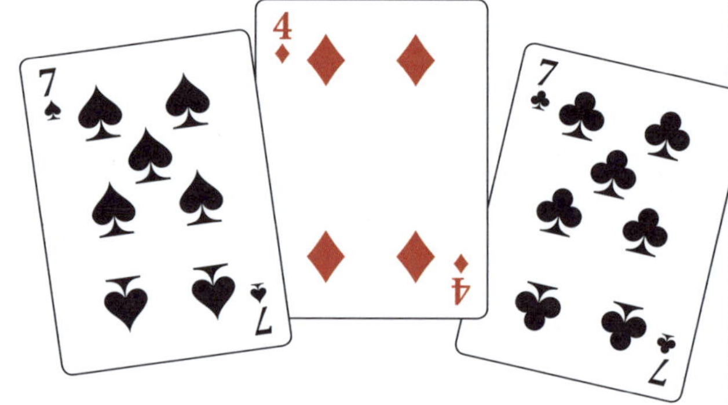

Clare chooses the two 7s and uses this key sequence on the calculator to find out how close she is to 50:

50 − 7 × 7 = 1

We practise

This is your hand in 'Closest to 50'.

Which two cards will you choose?

What calculator key sequence will tell you how close the product is to 50?

Check: 50 – 6 x 7 = 8

You practise

**These are your hands in 'Closest to 50'.
Choose two cards and write the calculator key sequence.**

Check: ____ – ____ × ____ = ____

Check: ____ – ____ × ____ = ____

Check: ____ – ____ × ____ = ____

Check: ____ – ____ × ____ = ____

Check: ____ – ____ × ____ = ____

Check: ____ – ____ × ____ = ____

Compare these two hands and decide who wins the point and why.

Jake

Clare

Who wins the point? ______________

Why? ____

BOB time!

MULTIPLYING MONEY

When you buy more than one of an item, it's handy to know how much the total cost will be. The best way to work out the cost is by multiplying.

For example, to buy 6 beads that are 5 cents each, you can count in **5 cents** six times.

      = 6 × 5¢ = 30¢

But you could work smarter and think in **10s**.

10 10 10

     = 3 × 10¢ = 30¢

When you think in coins, remember that there are 100 cents in a dollar.

To buy 4 muffins that are $3 each it helps to think in **dollars**.

    = 4 × $2 = $8

    = 4 × $1 = $4

$12

We practise

Show how to work out how much 3 beads at 35¢ each would cost by thinking in coins.

(5) x 3 = 15
(10) x 3 = 30
(20) x 3 = 60
→ $1·05

3 x 35¢ = $1·05

Show how to work out how much 5 pencils at $4·50 each would cost by thinking in dollars and cents.

($2) x 5 = 10
($2) x 5 = 10
(50) x 5 = 2·50
→ $22·50

5 x $4·50 = $22·50

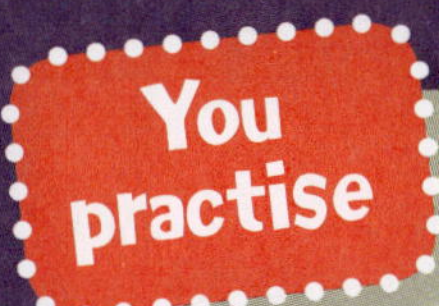

Show how to work out each amount by thinking in coins.

4 beads at 5¢ each

____ × ____ = ______

6 pencils at 10¢ each

____ × ____ = ______

7 erasers at 25¢ each

____ × ____ = ______

9 bread rolls at 35¢ each

____ × ____ = ______

Show how to work out each amount by thinking in dollars and cents.

3 subs at $4 each

____ × ____ = ______

4 muffins at $3·50 each

____ × ____ = ______

4 books at $6·20 each

____ × ____ = ______

5 books at $12·50 each

____ × ____ = ______

BOB time!

DIVISION

There are two types of division that you meet in everyday life. One kind is when you know how many groups to make, but you don't know how many to put in each group. Look at this example.

Clare has **12 cherries** to share **between 4 people**. How many cherries should each person get?

This can be written as **12 ÷ 4 = 3**.

Share the cherries into 4 equal-sized groups.

Put the cherries into groups of 3 and count how many groups you can make.

The other kind of division is when you know how many in each group, but you don't know how many groups you can make. Look at this example.

Clare has **12 cherries** to share and wants to give **each person 3 cherries**. How many people get cherries?

This can be written as **12 ÷ 3 = 4**.

We practise

Show how to share these cherries equally between 5 people and write the division sentence.

15 ÷ 5 = 3

Show how to give each person 4 cherries and write the division sentence.

16 ÷ 4 = 4

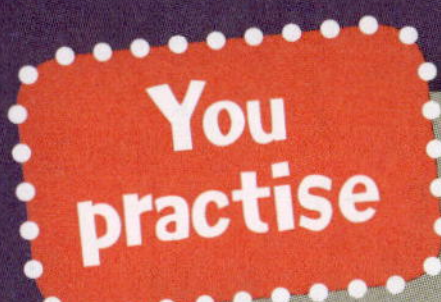

Show how to share these cherries equally and write the division sentence.

Share between 3 people

___ ÷ ___ = ___

Share between 4 people

___ ÷ ___ = ___

Share between 7 people

___ ÷ ___ = ___

Share between 10 people

___ ÷ ___ = ___

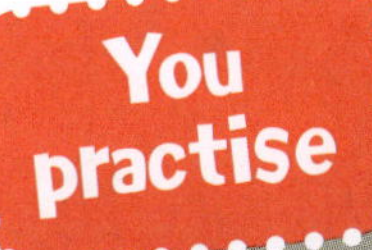

Show how to give each person an equal number of cherries and write the division sentence.

Share between 4 people

___ ÷ ___ = ___

Share between 5 people

___ ÷ ___ = ___

Share between 5 people

___ ÷ ___ = ___

Share between 7 people

___ ÷ ___ = ___

BOB time!

PROBLEM SOLVING

Marvellous Marbles

Clare shared her bag of 36 marbles between the 4 people in her team. How many marbles does each team member have?

Notice that the important information is highlighted in blue and what has to be found out is highlighted in pink.

One way to solve this problem is to **draw 4 bags** and share the marbles one by one into each bag.

36 ÷ 4 = 9. Each team member has 9 marbles.

If you don't know the multiplication, use number splitting:

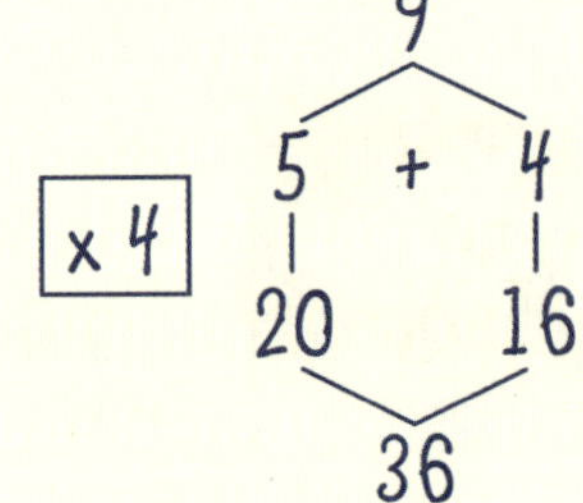

Another way is to **draw tallies**. This way requires less counting.

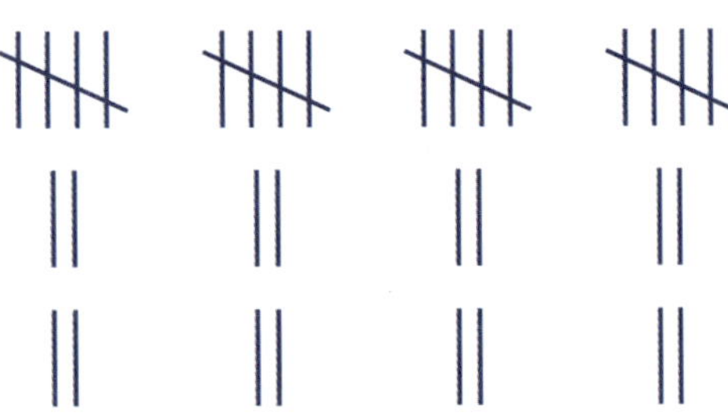

4 × **5** = 20

4 × **2** = 8 — **28**

8 left to share

4 × **2** = 8 — **36**

5 + 2 + 2 = 9. Each team member has 9 marbles.

Highlight the important information and what has to be found out in this problem. Write your answer as a sentence.

Jake made 4 bags of marbles with 9 marbles in each bag.

How many marbles did he start with?

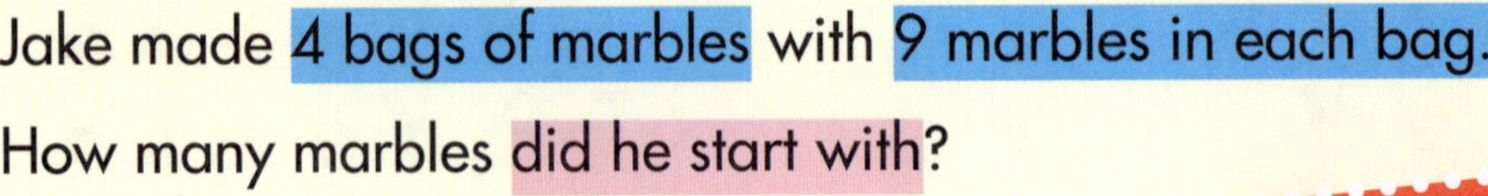

4 x 9 = 36

Answer: Jake started with 36 marbles.

You practise

Highlight the important information and what you have to find out. Write your answer as a sentence.

UNIT 10

1. Clare has 30 chocolate buttons to share equally to make six muffins. How many chocolate buttons for each muffin?

____

2. Clare threw a four on her dice six times in a row. What is her score?

____

3. Mum put six cherries into each of the six fruit salads. How many cherries did she use?

____

4. The muffins were packed in boxes of 12. There are four muffins in each row. How many rows are in the box?

____

5. When playing dominoes, four people each take seven dominoes. How many dominoes do they take altogether?

____

6. Muffins cost $3 each. How many muffins can Clare buy for $18?

____

7. "How can I share these 12 apples equally into three baskets?" Mum asked.

____

8. Dad gave $15 to Clare, Jake and Mary to share equally between them. How much do they each get?

____

9. Clare has three bags with four marbles in each. Jake has two bags with six marbles in each. Who has more?

____

10. Clare shared her marbles between three friends. She gave them 4 each. She still has 5 marbles for herself. How many marbles did she start with?

____

BOB time!

USING MULTIPLICATION FACTS for DIVISION

You can use multiplication facts to work out some divisions.

For example, to work out **24 ÷ 4**, you can use a multiplication fact that you already know: **4 × 6 = 24**.

4 rows of 6

This also tells you that 24 ÷ 4 = 6.

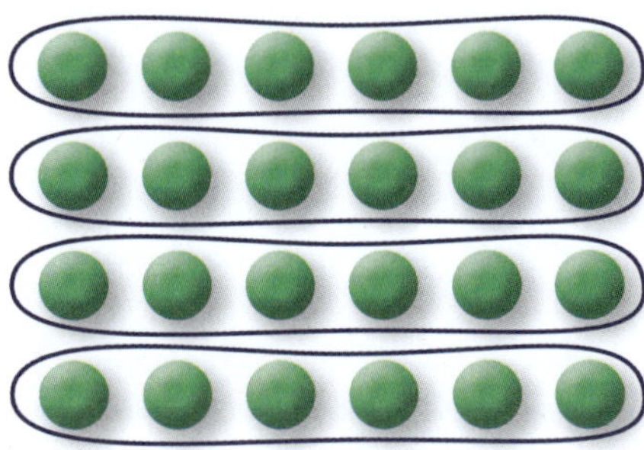

4 equal-sized groups of 6

4 × 6 = 24
6 × 4 = 24
24 ÷ 4 = 6
24 ÷ 6 = 4
These are all part of one fact family.

You can use this strategy to work out other divisions. Just ask yourself:

What is the multiplication fact that will help me?

For example, to work out 35 ÷ 5:

Ask: **5 × what = 35?**

Answer: **5 × 7 = 35, so 35 ÷ 5 = 7**

You can use the multiplication grid at the back of the book (page 52) to help you.

For 27 ÷ 3, find 27 in the column with 3 at the top. The number at the start of that row is the answer.

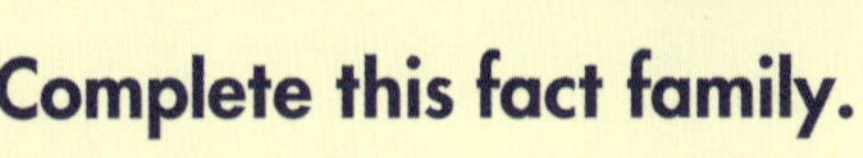

Complete this fact family.

4 × 3 = 12 12 ÷ 3 = 4
3 × 4 = 12 12 ÷ 4 = 3

Which multiplication fact helps with this division?

27 ÷ 3

3 × 9 = 27

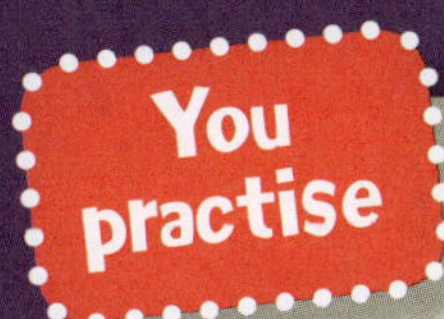

Complete each fact family.

5 × ____ = 30

____ × ____ = 30

30 ÷ ____ = ____

____ ÷ ____ = ____

4 × ____ = 24

____ × ____ = 24

24 ÷ ____ = ____

____ ÷ ____ = ____

3

8 × ____ = 32

____ × ____ = 32

32 ÷ ____ = ____

____ ÷ ____ = ____

6 × ____ = 42

____ × ____ = 42

42 ÷ ____ = ____

____ ÷ ____ = ____

Remember to use the **multiplication grid** at the back of the book if you need to.

You practise

Which multiplication fact helps with each division?

36 ÷ 6 = ____

6 × ____ = ____

54 ÷ 6 = ____

6 × ____ = ____

28 ÷ 4 = ____

4 × ____ = ____

45 ÷ 9 = ____

9 × ____ = ____

56 ÷ 7 = ____

7 × ____ = ____

72 ÷ 8 = ____

8 × ____ = ____

BOB time!

DOUBLES

Being able to **double** numbers is a very useful strategy for **multiplication**.

Number splitting and **chunking** are also really useful.

For example, to **double 18**, **split** 18 into **two chunks**, 10 and 8, then **double and add** the two parts.

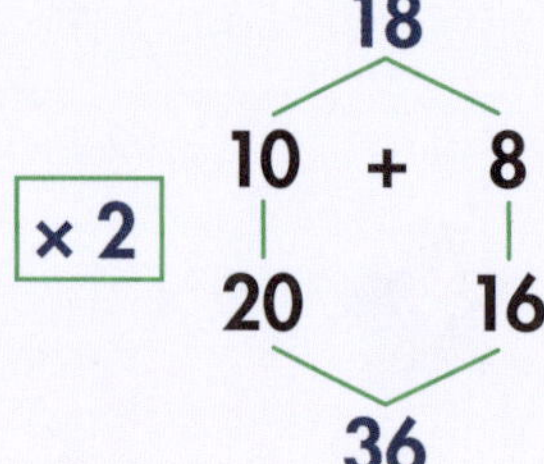

Did you know that **all the doubles** to double 10 are in the multiplication grid on page 52? They're in the 2 × row.

If you do the chunking **in your head**, then it's easy to double the chunks and you can leave out a step.

Even larger numbers are easy to deal with using this strategy.

57

× 2

50 + 7

100   14

114

We practise

Show how to double 36 using chunking.

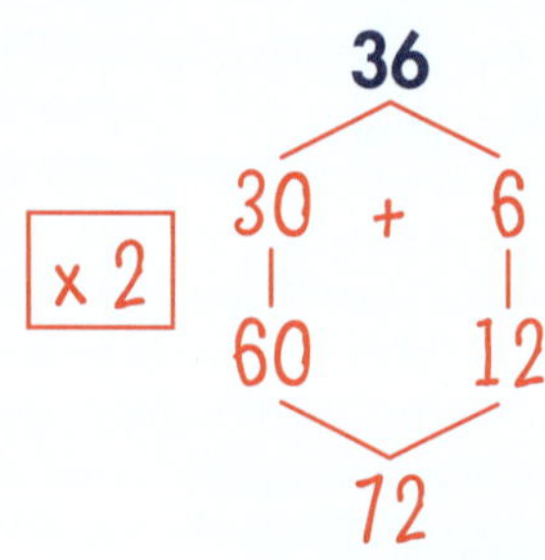

Show how to double 75, but do the chunking step in your head.

75

x 2   140 + 10

150

You practise Show how to double each number using chunking.

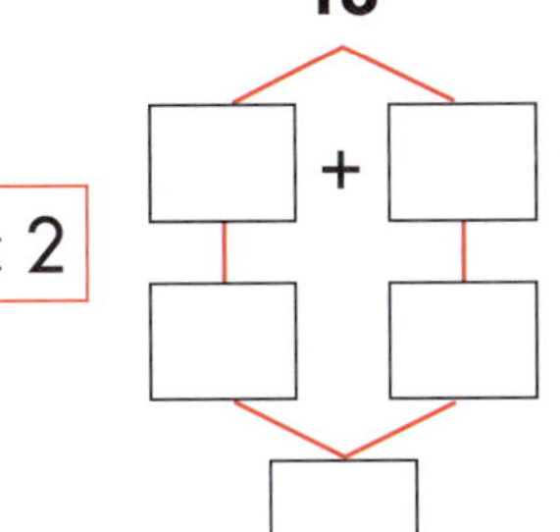

3

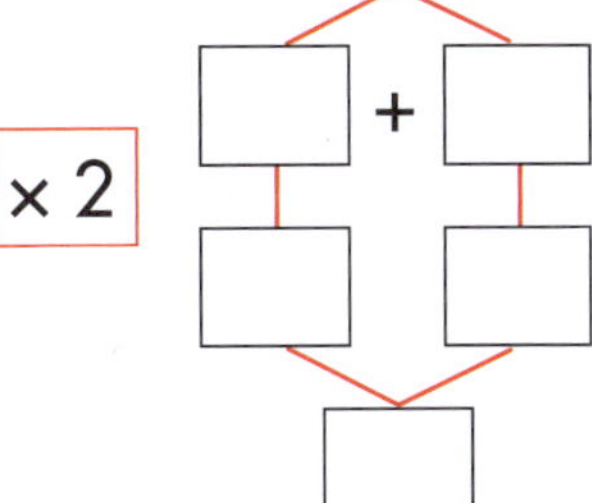

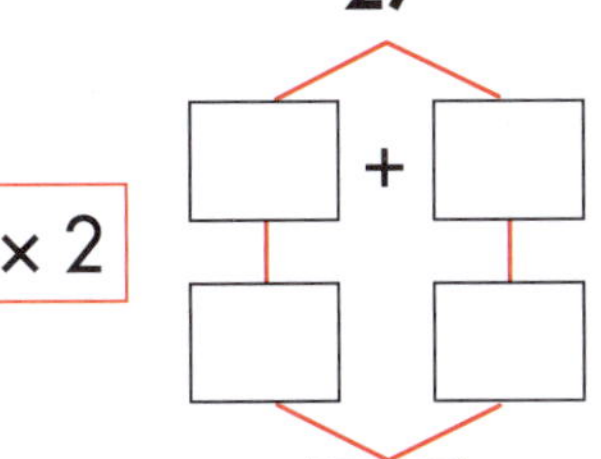

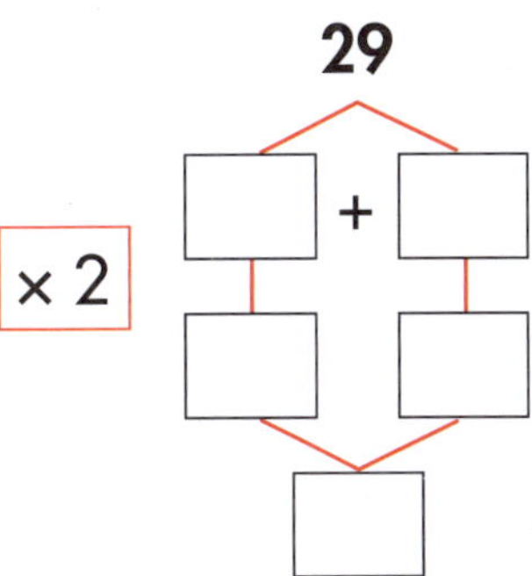

Show how to double each number, but do the chunking in your head.

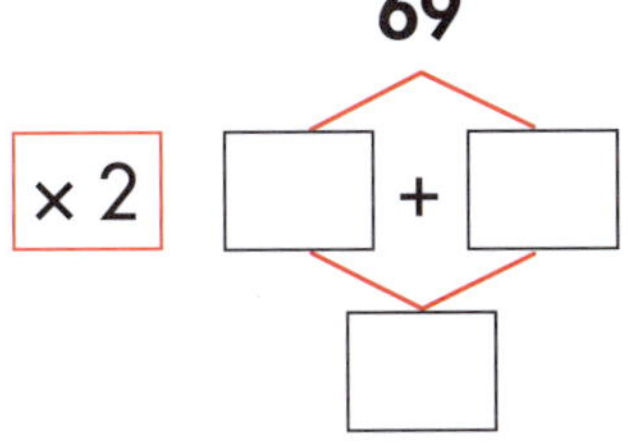

7

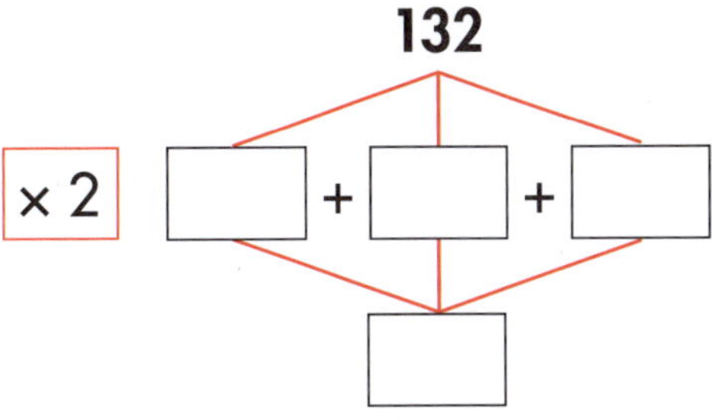

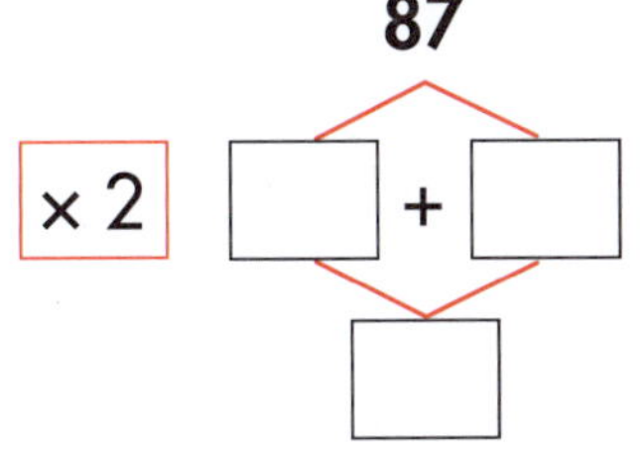

8

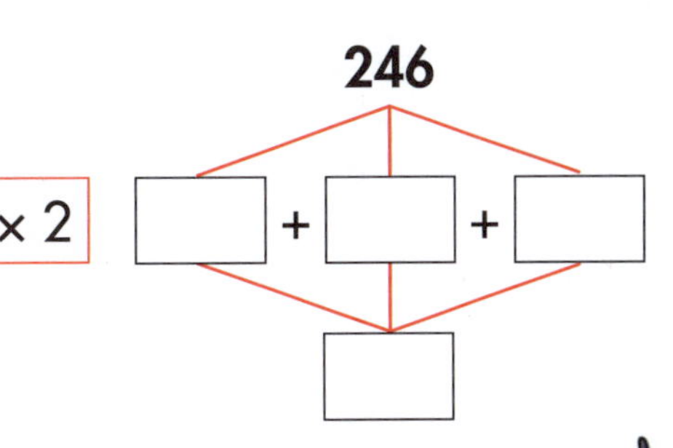

BOB time!

UNIT 13 HALVING

If you don't know half of 30, **split 30** into **20** and **10**. That makes it easy.

Being able to halve numbers is a very useful strategy for division.

Remember that **halving** is related to **doubling**.
You use the **2s multiplication facts** for both strategies.

For example, to **halve 18**, **split** 18 into **two chunks**, 10 and 8, then **halve** 10 and 8 and **add** the two parts.

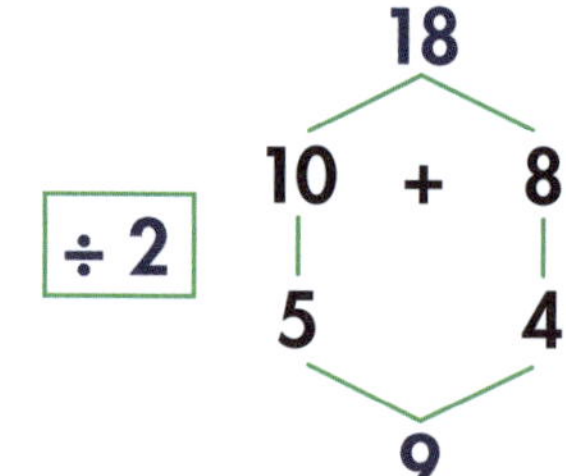

Even large numbers are easy to halve using chunking.

For example, here are two ways of **splitting and chunking 36**.

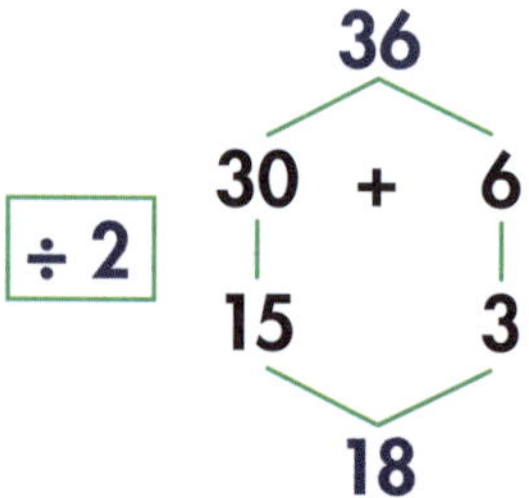

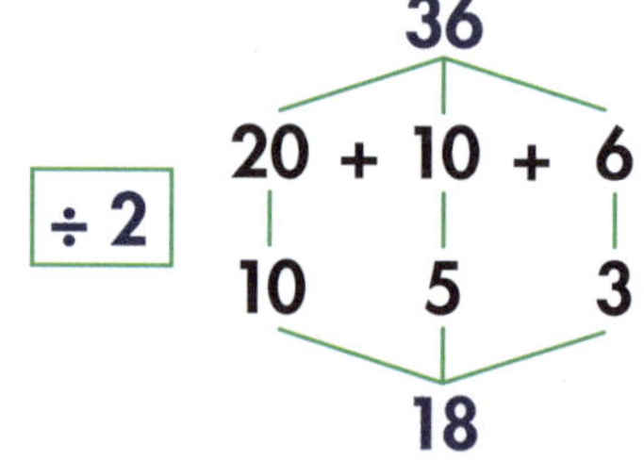

We practise

Show how to halve 26 using chunking.

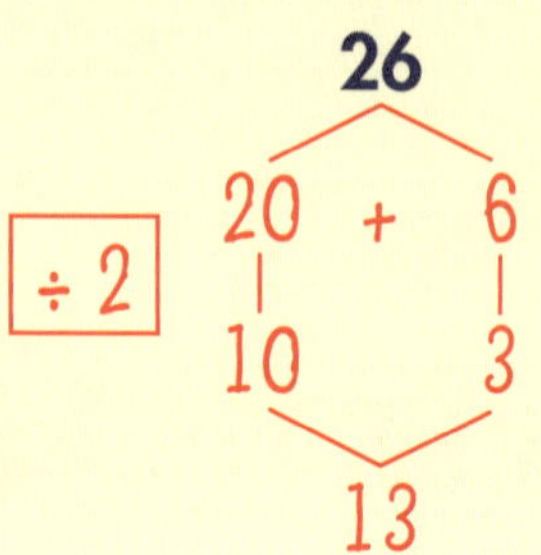

Show how to halve 56 using chunking into three parts.

56
÷ 2
40 + 10 + 6
20 5 3
28

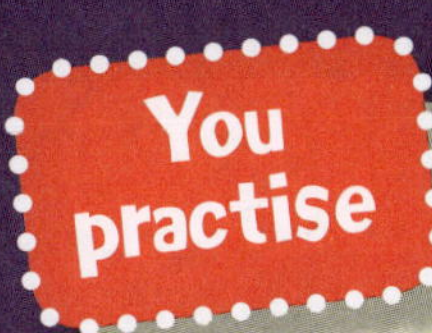

Show how to halve these numbers using chunking.

1. 28 (÷ 2)

3. 64 (÷ 2)

2. 46 (÷ 2)

4. 86 (÷ 2)

You practise

Show how to halve these numbers using chunking.

5. 38

7. 178

Chunk these numbers into 3 parts if you want to.

6. 78

8. 258

BOB time!

MULTIPLYING BY 10 and 100

10 is a friendly number, which means that it is easy to multiply by.

Look at these multiplications. Can you see a pattern that works for multiplying whole numbers?

6 × 10 = **60**
60 × 10 = **600**
600 × 10 = **6000**

This works for larger numbers too.
16 × 10 = 160

When you **count by 10s** from 0, there is always **one zero** in the 1s position.

0, 10, 20, 30, 40, 50, 60 ...

When you **count by 100s** from 0, there are always **two zeroes** at the end of each number – one in the 10s position and one in the 1s position.

0, 100, 200, 300, 400, 500, 600 ...

This helps you to understand why, when you **multiply by 10**, you just put one zero on the end of the number being multiplied.

However, you don't just add a zero when you multiply by 10.

Look at this place value diagram to see what happens when you **multiply 24 by 10**.

100s	10s	1s
	2	**4**
2	**4**	**0**

When you **multiply by 100**, each digit moves up two places, so you put two zeroes on the end of the number being multiplied, so **24 × 100 = 2400**.

We practise

Show what happens when you multiply these numbers by 10.

7 × 10 = 70

14 × 10 = 140

35 × 10 = 350

Show what happens when you multiply these numbers by 100.

7 × 100 = 700

12 × 100 = 1200

47 × 100 = 4700

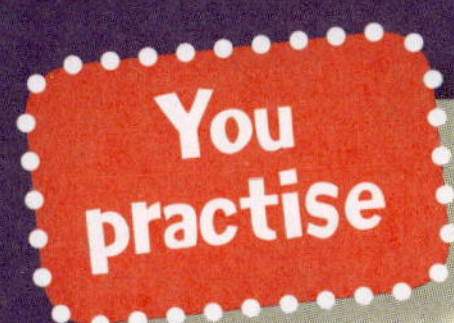

Answer these multiply by 10 questions.

8 × 10 = ________

4 × 10 = ________

10 × 7 = ________

4 12 × 10 = ________

5 14 × 10 = ________

70 × 10 = ________

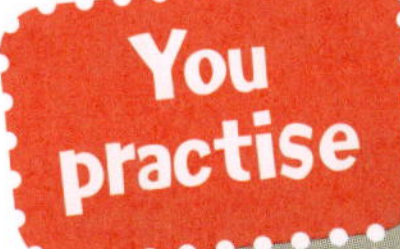

Answer these multiply by 100 questions.
Have a go at the multiply by 1000 questions.

8 × 100 = ________

12 × 100 = ________

60 × 100 = ________

100 × 100 = ________

6 × 1000 = ________

1000 × 23 = ________

BOB time!

MULTIPLICATION OF TWO-DIGIT NUMBERS

When you **multiply a two-digit number**, a good strategy is to use **number splitting** and **chunking**. Here is an example.

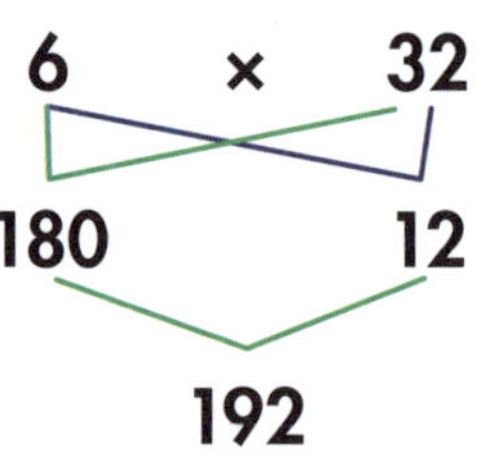

You can do the same multiplication using the **front-end method**.

Using this method, you multiply the **10s part** of the two-digit number first and then multiply the **1s part**. Look at this example.

$$\begin{array}{r} 32 \\ \times \quad 6 \\ \hline 180 \\ 12 \\ \hline 192 \\ \hline \end{array} \qquad \begin{array}{r} \\ \\ 30 \times 6 = 180 \\ 2 \times 6 = 12 \\ \\ \end{array}$$

We practise

Show how to use chunking to work out this multiplication.

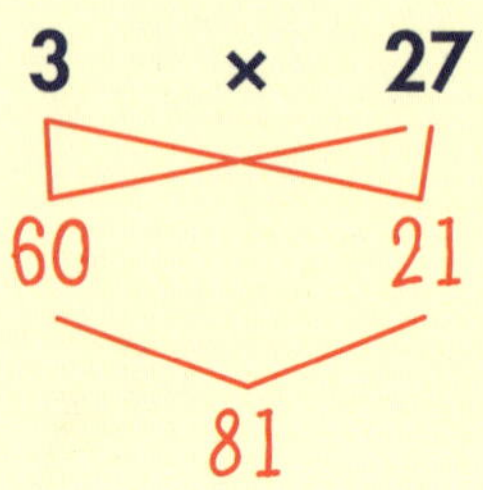

Show how to use the front-end method to work out this multiplication.

$$\begin{array}{r} 27 \\ \times \quad 3 \\ \hline 60 \\ 21 \\ \hline 81 \\ \hline \end{array} \qquad \begin{array}{r} \\ \\ 3 \times 20 = 60 \\ 3 \times 7 = 21 \\ \\ \end{array}$$

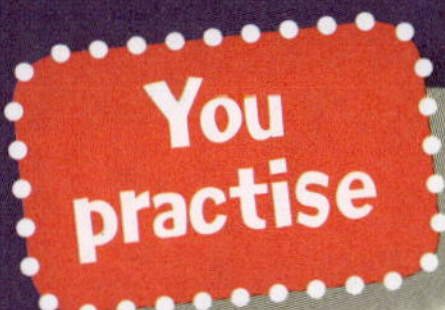

Use chunking to work out each multiplication.

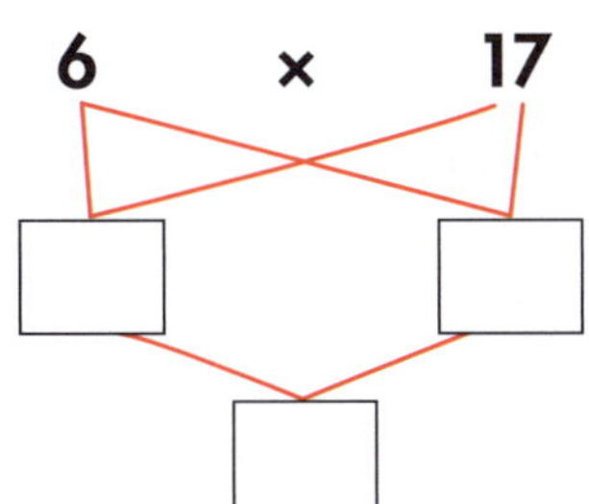

3

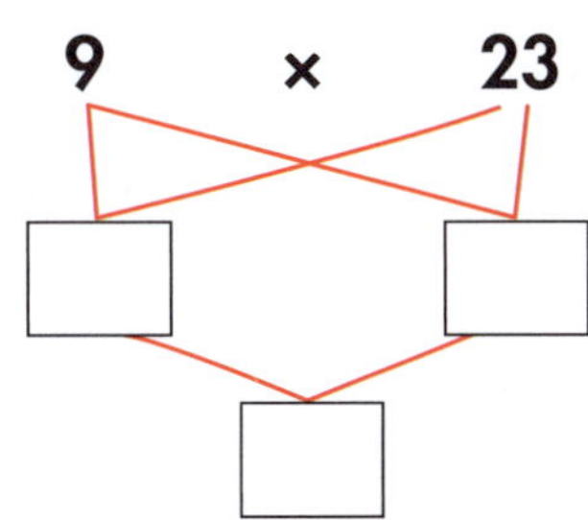

2

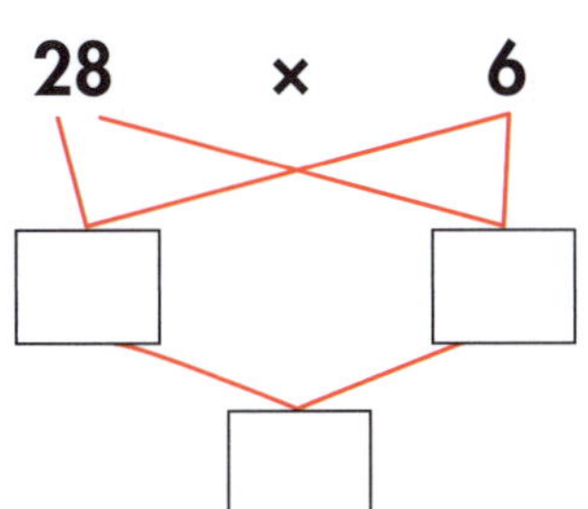

4

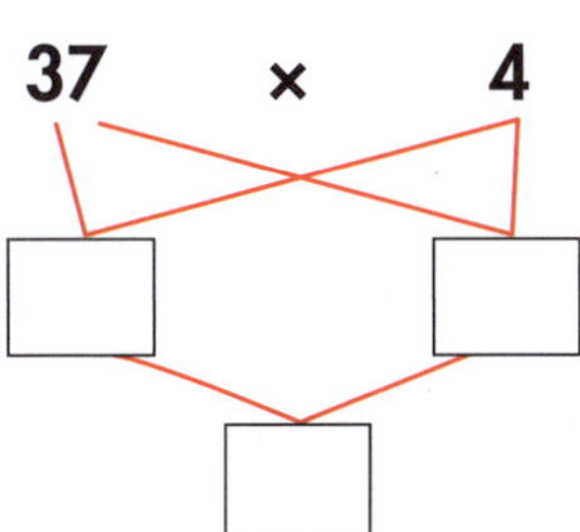

You practise

Use the front-end method to work out each multiplication.

$$\begin{array}{r} 37 \\ \times \quad 4 \\ \hline \end{array}$$

$$\begin{array}{r} 46 \\ \times \quad 8 \\ \hline \end{array}$$

$$\begin{array}{r} 54 \\ \times \quad 7 \\ \hline \end{array}$$

$$\begin{array}{r} 58 \\ \times \quad 9 \\ \hline \end{array}$$

BOB time!

SMART WAY to MULTIPLY by 5

One smart way to **multiply by 5** is to use your **10s multiplication facts** followed by **halving**.

Look at this easy example.

5 × 7

Step 1	Multiply by 10:	10 × 7 = 70
Step 2	Halve the result:	35
Answer:		5 × 7 = 35

Check the answer with a **calculator** to see if it is correct.

Let's try it with a larger number.

5 × 36

Step 1	Multiply by 10:	10 × 36 = 360
Step 2	Halve the result:	180
Answer:		5 × 36 = 180

We practise

Show how to use a 10s multiplication fact and halving strategy to work out 14 × 5.

Step 1: 14 × 10 = 140

Step 2: Halve 140 = 70

Answer: 14 × 5 = 70

What is the 5s multiplication in this example?

Step 1: 17 × 10 = 170

Step 2: Halve 170 = 85

Multiplication: 17 × 5 = 85

You practise

Show how to use a 10s multiplication fact and halving strategy to work out each multiplication.

5 × 24

Step 1: ____________________

Step 2: ____________________

Answer: ____ × ____ = ____

5 × 48

Step 1: ____________________

Step 2: ____________________

Answer: ____ × ____ = ____

3 38 × 5

Step 1: ____________________

Step 2: ____________________

Answer: ____ × ____ = ____

68 × 5

Step 1: ____________________

Step 2: ____________________

Answer: ____ × ____ = ____

What is the 5s multiplication in each example?

Step 1: 10 × 68 = 680

Step 2: Halve 680 = 340

Multiplication: ____ × ____ = ____

Step 1: 10 × 26 = 260

Step 2: Halve 260 = 130

Multiplication: ____ × ____ = ____

Step 1: 10 × 37 = 370

Step 2: Halve 370 = ____

Multiplication: ____ × ____ = ____

Step 1: 10 × 79 = 790

Step 2: Halve 790 = ____

Multiplication: ____ × ____ = ____

Sometimes you don't need to halve, but you should always check the answer on your calculator.

BOB time!

UNIT 17

DIVIDING BY 10

When you divide a number by 10 it has the opposite effect to when you multiply a number by 10.

Look at these examples.

70 ÷ 10 = 7

350 ÷ 10 = 35

500 ÷ 10 = 50

4000 ÷ 10 = 400

So when you **divide by 10**, instead of adding an extra zero at the end of the number – as you do when you multiply – you **remove a zero**.

Look at this place value diagram to see what happens when you divide **350 by 10**.

100s	10s	1s
3	5	0
	3	5

Did you notice that there is one less zero every time you divide by 10?

Look what happens when you divide by 100.

500 ÷ 100 = 5

1200 ÷ 100 = 12

7000 ÷ 100 = 70

90 000 ÷ 100 = 900

Two zeroes are removed this time!

We practise

Complete each division.

180 ÷ 10 = 18

2400 ÷ 10 = 240

55 000 ÷ 10 = 5500

1900 ÷ 100 = 19

25 000 ÷ 100 = 250

360 000 ÷ 100 = 3600

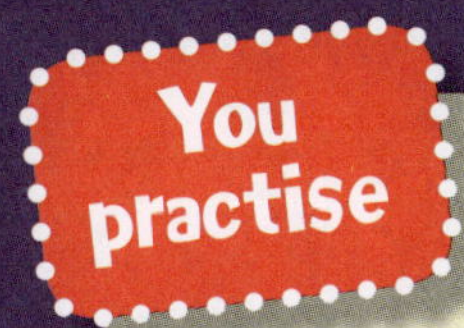

Complete each division.

170 ÷ 10 = __________

260 ÷ 10 = __________

340 ÷ 10 = __________

390 ÷ 10 = __________

3 600 ÷ 100 = __________

4 800 ÷ 100 = __________

7 80 000 ÷ 100 = __________

8 910 000 ÷ 100 = __________

3 600 ÷ 10 = __________

10 4 700 ÷ 100 = __________

11 56 000 ÷ 100 = __________

48 000 ÷ 1 000 = __________

BOB time!

UNIT 18

DIVIDING TWO-DIGIT NUMBERS

The **number splitting** strategy that you used for **halving** also works well for **division** by other numbers.

For example, to find **36 ÷ 3**, **split 36** into 30 + 6. These numbers were chosen because they are easy to divide by 3.

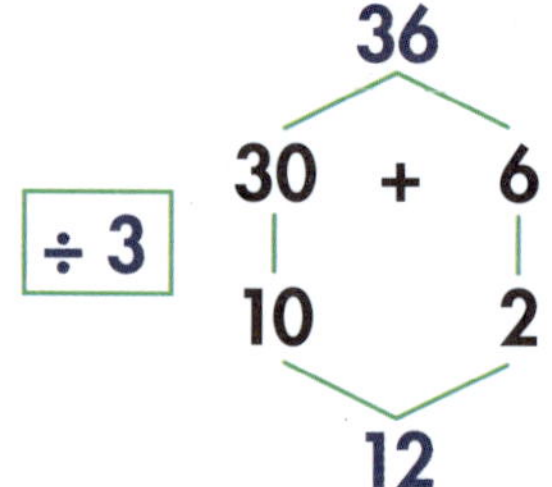

36 ÷ 3 = 12

Let's try 56 ÷ 4 this time.

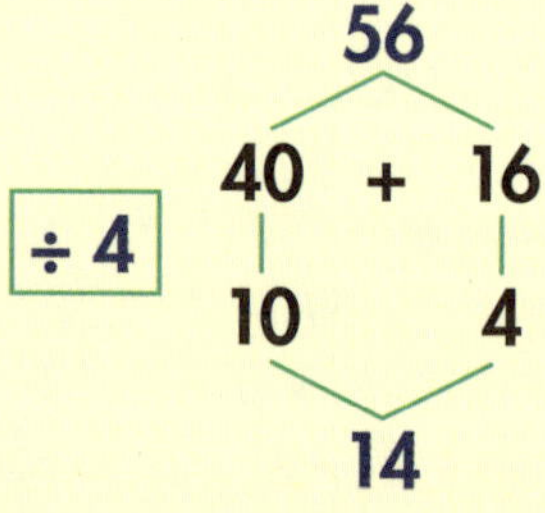

56 ÷ 4 = 14

You know that

so split 56 into 40 + 16.

We practise

Show how you would split 42 so that it is easy to divide by 3.

42

30 + 12

Use the number splitting strategy to work out 72 ÷ 6.

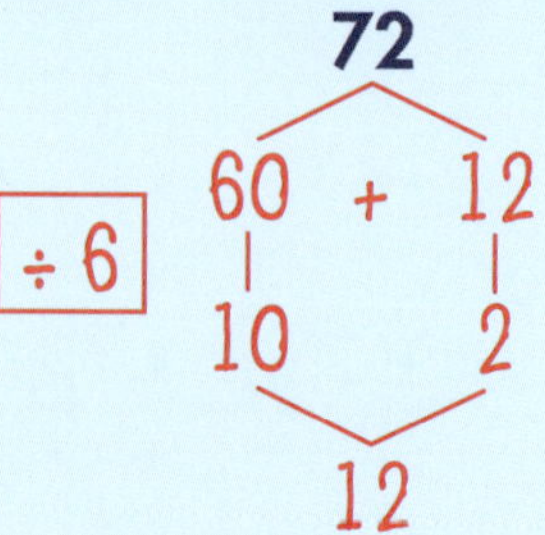

You practise Show how you would split each number to make it easy to divide.

1. 24 ÷ 4

24

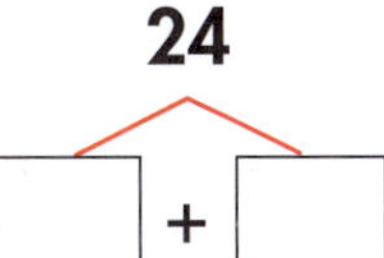

2. 84 ÷ 7

84

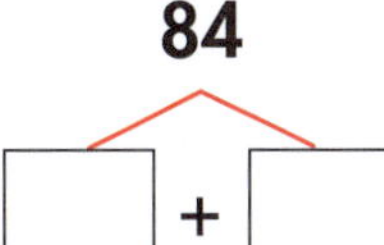

3. 65 ÷ 5

65

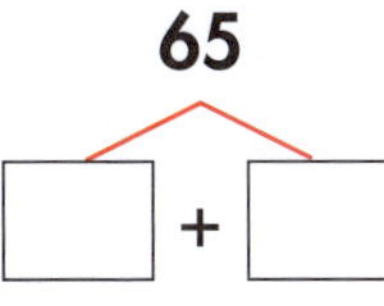

4. 48 ÷ 6

48

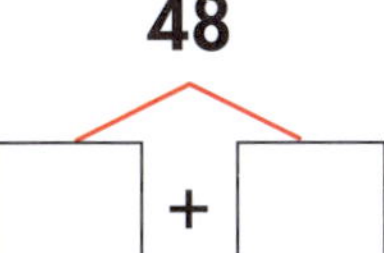

Knowing **5s and 10s facts** helps with these divisions.

You practise Use the number splitting strategy to work out each division.

5. 39 ÷ 3

39

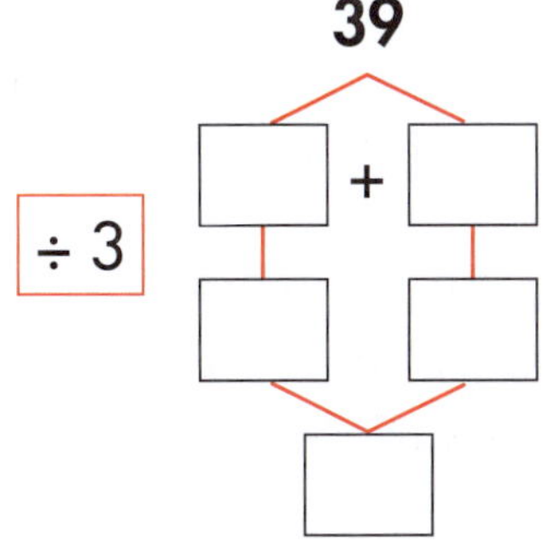

6. 108 ÷ 9

108

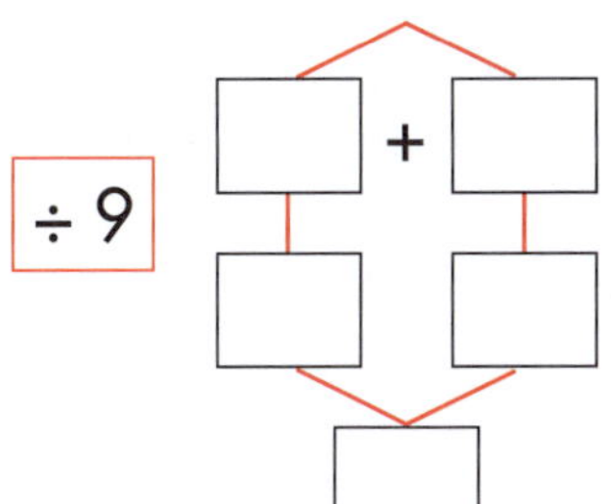

7. 126 ÷ 6

126

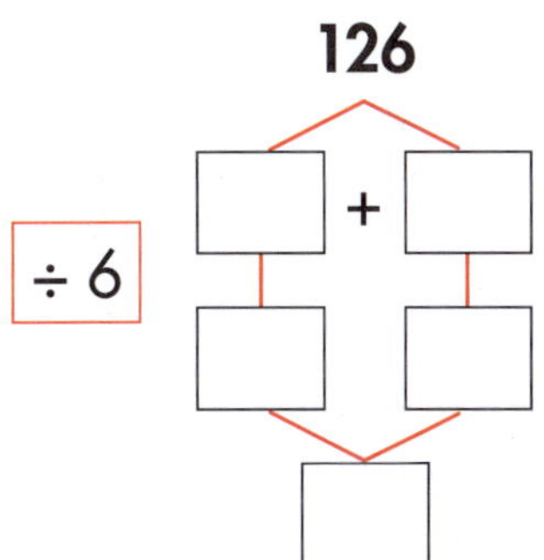

8. 125 ÷ 5

125

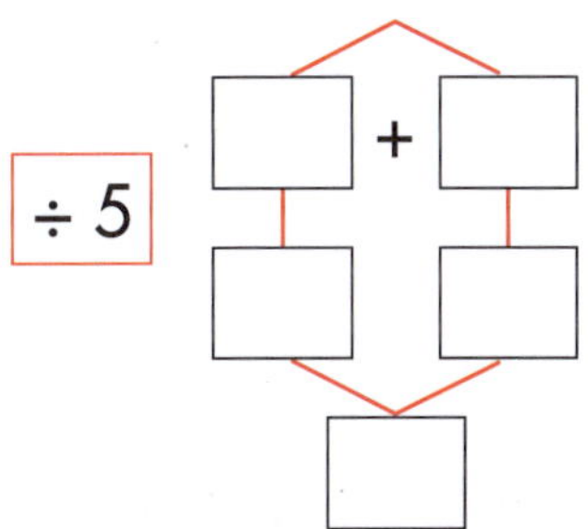

BOB time!

LONG DIVISION

I have **162 jellybeans** in my jar and I want to make bags with **6 jellybeans in each bag**. **How many bags** of jellybeans can I make?

Here is an easy way to work out this problem using **long division**.

```
     2 7 bags
6 ) 1 6 2
  -   6 0    10 bags of 6 = 60, so take out 60 jellybeans
    1 0 2
  -   6 0    10 bags of 6 = 60, so take out 60 jellybeans
      4 2
  -   4 2    7 bags of 6 = 42, so take out 42 jellybeans
        0    jellybeans remaining
             Add the bags: 10 + 10 + 7 = 27 bags
```

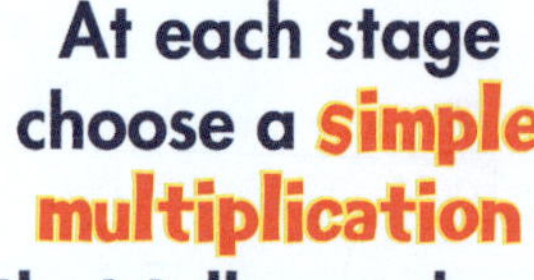

At each stage choose a **simple multiplication** that tells you how many jellybeans to take out of the jar.

We practise

Use long division to work out how many bags can be made out of 84 jellybeans with 6 jellybeans in each bag.

```
    1 4 bags
6 ) 8 4
  - 6 0    10 bags of 6 = 60
    2 4
  - 2 4    4 bags of 6 = 24
      0
           10 + 4 = 14 bags
```

Use long division to work out how many marbles in each bag if 112 marbles are divided equally into 8 bags.

```
      1 4 bags
8 ) 1 1 2
  -   8 0    10 bags of 8 = 80
      3 2
  -   3 2    4 bags of 8 = 32
        0
             10 + 4 = 14 bags
```

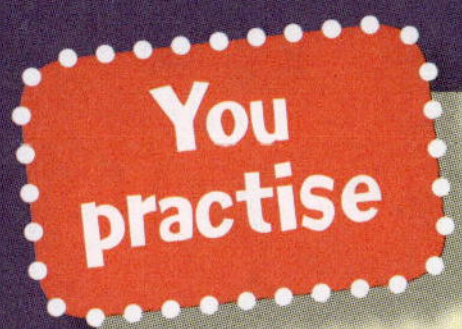

Show how to solve each division using long division.

$4\overline{)76}$

$9\overline{)117}$

Remember to choose a **simple multiplication** at each stage.

$5\overline{)115}$

$6\overline{)132}$

$7\overline{)91}$

$7\overline{)154}$

$8\overline{)168}$

$8\overline{)176}$

BOB time!

MORE PROBLEM SOLVING

The button factory sews 8 buttons on to a card because buttons are most frequently used 8 at a time. They have made 152 buttons in the first batch for today.

How many cards will they be able to make?

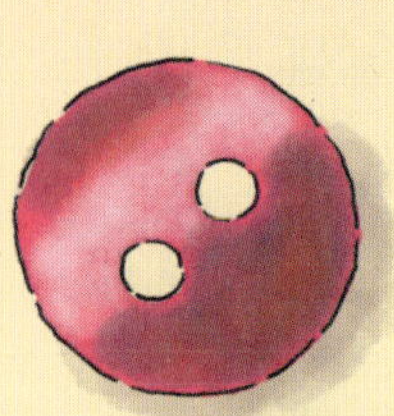

Now for the working out! If there are 8 buttons on each card, you need to find 152 ÷ 8. You can use long division to work this out.

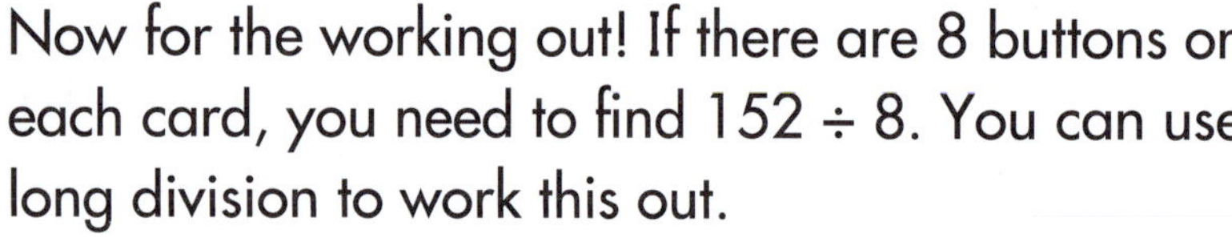

```
      1 9  cards
  8 ) 1 5 2
    –   8 0    10 cards of 8 = 80
        7 2
    –   7 2    9 cards of 8 = 72
          0
               10 + 9 = 19 cards
```

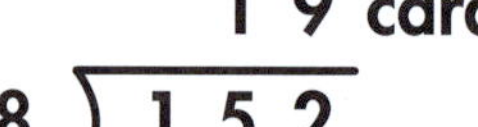

Answer: The factory will be able to make 19 cards of buttons.

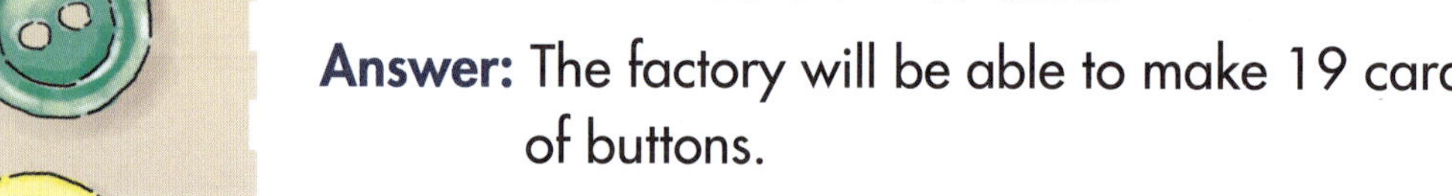

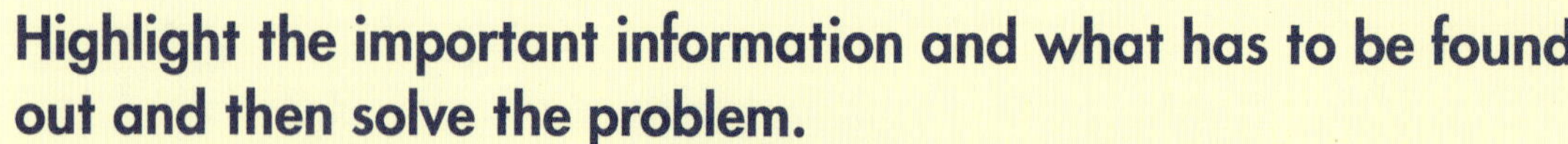

Highlight the important information and what has to be found out and then solve the problem.

Jake and Clare want to put 112 marbles into bags of 7 ready for the marbles tournament. How many bags will they be able to make?

```
      1 6  bags
  7 ) 1 1 2
    –   7 0    10 bags of 7 = 70
        4 2
    –   4 2    6 bags of 7 = 42
          0
               10 + 6 = 16 bags
```

Answer: Jake and Clare will be able to make 16 bags of marbles.

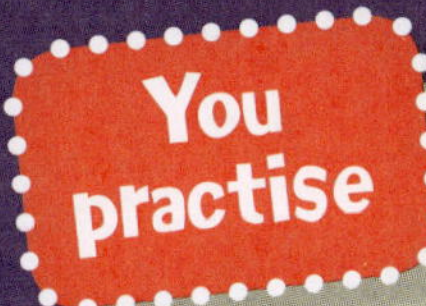

Highlight the important information and what has to be found out and then solve the problem.

Tsai made 32 radishes into bunches of 8. How many bunches does she make?

____

Matty made seven bunches of six radishes. How many radishes does he have?

____

Clare's savings doubled 3 times this month because she was doing odd jobs. She started with $7. How much does she have now?

____

Jake played four games of marbles. Each round he lost half his marbles. He started with sixty-four marbles. How many marbles did he have left?

____

Jake threw 6 on the dice and then multiplied by 10 and then by 100. What number did Jake make?

____

Clare threw six on the dice and then multiplied it by ten three times. What number did Clare make?

____

Each bus carries 64 passengers. The school filled 4 buses when they went to a concert. How many people went to the concert?

____

The school wants to take 2 classes each with 24 children and 2 adults to the zoo. A minibus holds 13 people. How many minibuses do they need to book?

____

The jar of 128 jellybeans is to be made into bags of 8 jellybeans. How many bags can be made?

____

Jake says he knows a really quick way of working out 5 × 36. What could it be?

____

BOB time!

TEST 1

Write two multiplication sentences that show how many biscuits are in the packet.

____ × ____ = ____

____ × ____ = ____

Write the multiplication sentence for these tallies.

卌 卌 卌 卌
|| || || ||

____ × ____ = ____

Write the multiplication sentence for this problem.

There were 6 flowers in a vase. Each flower has seven petals. How many petals were there altogether?

____ × ____ = ____

How many equal-sized jumps of 6 are needed to land on 36? Show how to work this out on the number line.

Start

____ × ____ = ____

Complete these two related number sentences.

____ × 4 = 24

____ × ____ = 24

Estimate and then check to work out 3 × 9.

Estimate: ____ × 10 = ____

so ____ × ____ = ____

If you sell six plants at 45¢ each, how much money will you make?

____

Show how to share these cherries fairly between six people and write the division sentence.

____ ÷ ____ = ____

Each of our 7 hens laid 6 eggs last week. How many eggs altogether?

____

I need to give six counters each to a group of 6 students. How many counters do I need?

____

TEST 2

1. Complete this multiplication fact family.

   7 × ____ = 28

   ____ × ____ = 28

   28 ÷ ____ = ____

   ____ ÷ ____ = ____

2. Which multiplication fact helps with 36 ÷ 9?

   ____ × ____ = ____

3. Complete this diagram to double 76.

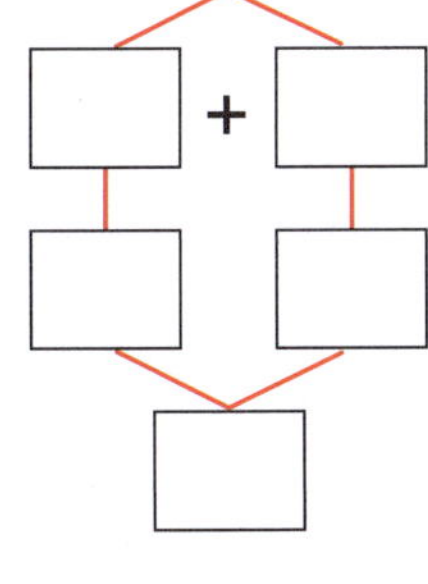

4. Complete this diagram to find half of 74.

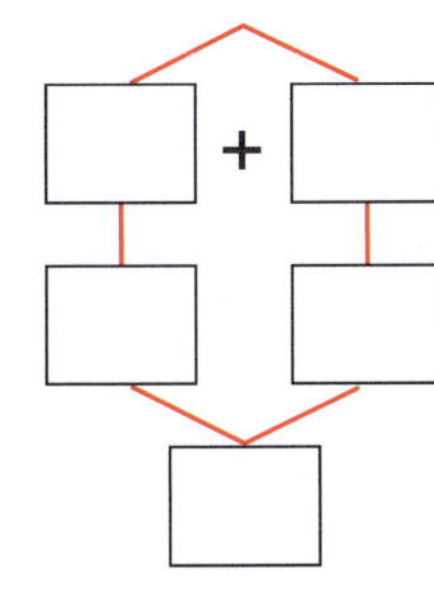

5. 75 × 10 = ____

   120 × 100 = ____

6. Work out 306 ÷ 9 using long division.

   $9\overline{)306}$

7. What is a quick way to work out 5 × 26?

   ____

8. 1300 ÷ 10 = ____

9. Show how to work out 72 ÷ 6 using number splitting.

10. There are 11 boys, 14 girls and 1 teacher in the classroom.

    How many toes are there altogether in the classroom?

    ____

ANSWERS

Unit 1

1 2 x 5 = 10, 5 x 2 = 10
2 3 x 6 = 18, 6 x 3 = 18
3 4 x 5 = 20, 5 x 4 = 20
4 3 x 7 = 21, 7 x 3 = 21
5 16
4 x 4 = 16
6 35
5 x 7 = 35

Unit 2

1 24
2 35
3 24
4 30
5 24
6 40
7 39
8 60

Unit 3

1 5 × 4 = 20
2 3 × 6 = 18
3 4 × 8 = 32
4 5 × 8 = 40
5 Repeated addition: 11 + 11 + 11 + 11
Multiplication: 4 × 11 = 44

Unit 4

1
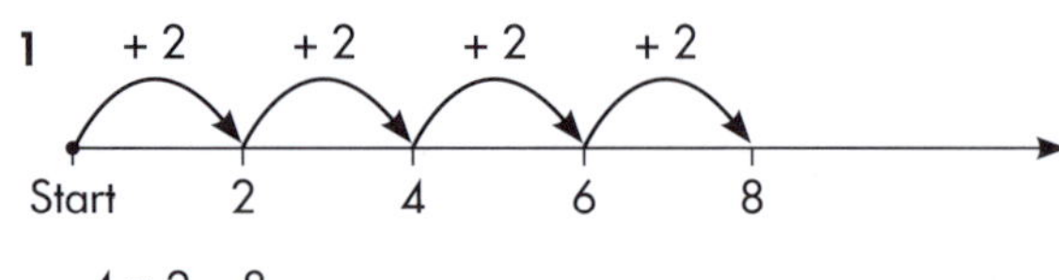

4 × 2 = 8

2
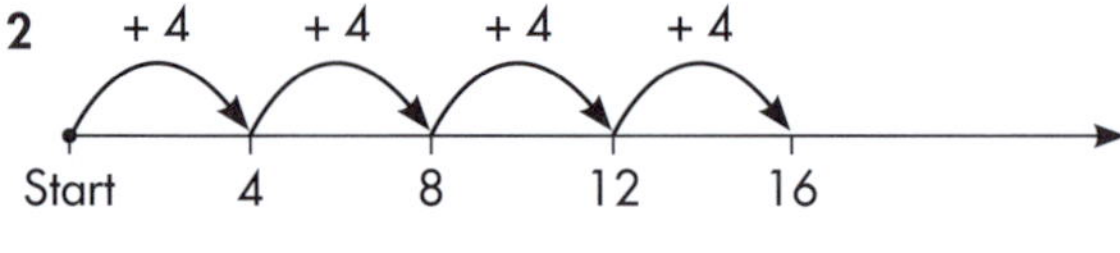

4 × 4 = 16

3
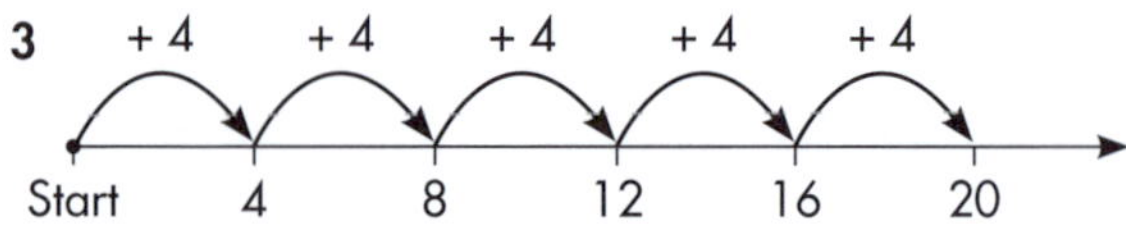

5 × 4 = 20. So 4 more jumps.

4 5 × 4 = 20
5 5
6 7
7 11
8 4

Unit 5

1 6 × 4 = 24
2 4 × 5 = 20
3 6 × 5 = 30
4 8 × 4 = 32
5 7 × 5 = 35, 5 × 7 = 35
6 4 × 9 = 36, 9 × 4 = 36
7 4 × 6 = 24, 6 × 4 = 24
8 6 × 10 = 60, 10 × 6 = 60
9 3 × 9 = 27, 9 × 3 = 27
10 4 × 7 = 28, 7 × 4 = 28
or 2 × 14 = 28, 14 × 2 = 28

Unit 6

1 Check 21
2 Check 36
3 Check 42
4 Check 56
5 Check 72
6 Check 64
7 Check 49
8 Check 54

Unit 7

1 50 – 5 × 8 = 10
2 50 – 6 × 7 = 8
3 50 – 5 × 6 = 20
4 50 – 5 × 9 = 5
5 50 – 6 × 9 = –4
6 50 – 5 × 10 = 0
7 Neither; both are 22 away from 50

Unit 8

1 4 × 5¢ = 20¢
2 6 × 10¢ = 60¢
3 7 x 25c = $1.75
4 9 × 35¢ = $3.15
5 3 × $4 = $12
6 4 × $3.50 = $14
7 4 × $6.20 = $24.80
8 $62.50

Unit 9

1 12 ÷ 3 = 4
2 21 ÷ 7 = 3
3 20 ÷ 4 = 5
4 20 ÷ 10 = 2
5 16 ÷ 4 = 4
6 30 ÷ 6 = 5
7 20 ÷ 5 = 4
8 35 ÷ 7 = 5

ANSWERS

Unit 10

1 5 chocolate buttons for each muffin
2 Clare's score is 24
3 She used 36 cherries
4 3 rows in the box
5 The take 28 dominoes altogether
6 She can buy 6 muffins
7 Put four 4 apples into each basket
8 They each get $5
9 Neither, they both have 12 marbles
10 She started with 17 marbles

Unit 11

1 $5 \times 6 = 30$, $6 \times 5 = 30$, $30 \div 5 = 6$, $30 \div 6 = 5$
2 $4 \times 6 = 24$, $6 \times 4 = 24$, $24 \div 6 = 4$, $24 \div 4 = 6$
3 $8 \times 4 = 32$, $4 \times 8 = 32$, $32 \div 4 = 8$, $32 \div 8 = 4$
4 $6 \times 7 = 42$, $7 \times 6 = 42$, $42 \div 6 = 7$, $42 \div 7 = 6$
5 $36 \div 6 = 6$, $6 \times 6 = 36$
6 $54 \div 6 = 9$, $6 \times 9 = 54$
7 $28 \div 4 = 7$, $4 \times 7 = 28$
8 $45 \div 9 = 5$, $9 \times 5 = 45$
9 $56 \div 7 = 8$, $7 \times 8 = 56$
10 $72 \div 8 = 9$, $8 \times 9 = 72$

Unit 12

1	10	+	8		
	20		16		
		36			
2	20	+	7		
	40		14		
		54			
3	50	+	3		
	100		6		
		106			
4	20	+	9		
	40		18		
		58			
5	120	+	18		
		138			
6	160	+	14		
		174			
7	200	+	60	+	4
			264		
8	400	+	80	+	12
			492		

Unit 13

1	20	+	8		
	10		4		
		14			
2	40	+	6		
	20		3		
		23			
3	60	+	4		
	30		2		
		32			
4	80	+	6		
	40		3		
		43			
5	30	+	8		
	15		4		
		19			
6	70	+	8		
	35		4		
		39			
7	100	+	70	+	8
	50		35		4
			89		
8	200	+	50	+	8
	100		25		4
			129		

Unit 14

1 80
2 40
3 70
4 120
5 140
6 700
7 800
8 1200
9 6000
10 10 000
11 6000
12 23 000

ANSWERS

Unit 15

1. 60 42
   102
2. 120 48
   168
3. 180 27
   207
4. 120 28
   148
5.
   1 2 0
   2 8
   1 4 8
6.
   3 5 0
   2 8
   3 7 8
7.
   3 2 0
   4 8
   3 6 8
8.
   4 5 0
   7 2
   5 2 2

Unit 16

1. 10 × 24 = 240
   Halve 240 = 120
   5 × 24 = 120
2. 10 × 48 = 480
   Halve 480 = 240
   5 × 48 = 240
3. 38 × 10 = 380
   Halve 380 = 190
   38 × 5 = 190
4. 68 × 10 = 680
   Halve 680 = 340
   68 × 5 = 340
5. 5 × 68 = 340
6. 5 × 26 = 130
7. 185, 5 × 37 = 185
8. 395, 5 × 79 = 395

Unit 17

1. 17
2. 26
3. 34
4. 39
5. 36
6. 48
7. 800
8. 9100
9. 360
10. 47
11. 560
12. 48

Unit 18

1. 20 + 4
2. 70 + 14
3. 50 + 15
4. 30 + 18
5. 30 + 9
   10 + 3
   13
6. 90 + 18
   10 + 2
   12
7. 120 + 6
   20 + 1
   21
8. 100 + 25
   20 + 5
   25

Unit 19

1. 19
2. 23
3. 13
4. 21
5. 13
6. 22
7. 22
8. 22

Unit 20

1. Tsai made 4 bunches
2. Matty has 42 radishes
3. Clare has saved $56
4. Jake has 8 marbles left
5. Jake made 6000
6. Clare made 6000
7. 256 people went to the concert
8. They need 4 minibuses
9. 16 bags of jellybeans
10. 5 × 30 + 5 × 6 = 150 + 30 = 180

ANSWERS

Test 1

1 3 x 5 = 15, 5 x 3 = 15

2 4 x 5 + 4 x 2 = 28

3 6 x 7 = 42

4

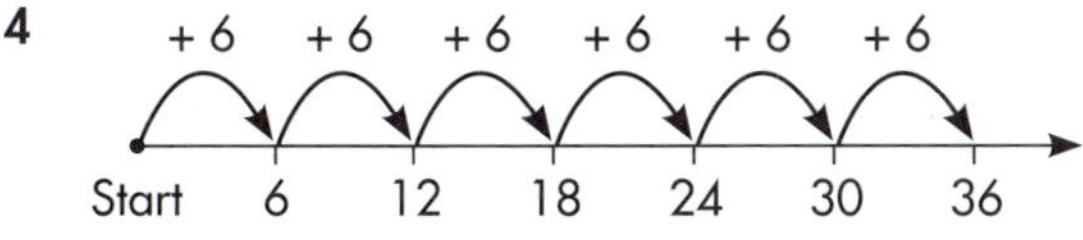

5 6 x 4 = 24, 4 x 6 = 24

6 Estimate: 3 × 10 = 30, so 3 × 9 = 27

7 6 × 45¢ = $2.70

8 18 ÷ 6 = 3

9 7 x 6 = 42

10 6 x 6 = 36

Test 2

1 7 × 4 = 28, 4 × 7 = 28, 28 ÷ 4 = 7, 28 ÷ 7 = 4

2 4 × 9 = 36

3 70 + 6
140 + 12
152

4 70 + 4
5 + 2
37

5 750, 12 000

6 34

7 10 × 26 = 260, halved = 130

8 1300 ÷ 10 = 130

9 60 + 12
10 + 2
12

10 26 × 10 = 260 toes altogether

Back to Basics Multiplication and Division Years 3–4

Reprinted 2016, 2018, 2023

ISBN: 978 1 74215 938 6

Published by Pascal Press
PO Box 250
Glebe NSW 2037
www.pascalpress.com.au
contact@pascalpress.com.au

Author: Ann Baker
Publisher: Lynn Dickinson
Editor: Eliza Hope
Proofreaders: Tim Learner, Ruth Schultz
Design and illustration: Janice Bowles
Page layout and technical illustration: Ruth Schultz
Cover design: Deb Snibson, MAPG
Printed by Wai Man Book Binding (China) Ltd.

Multiplication Grid

×	0	1	2	3	4	5	6	7	8	9	10
0	0	0	0	0	0	0	0	0	0	0	0
1	0	1	2	3	4	5	6	7	8	9	10
2	0	2	4	6	8	10	12	14	16	18	20
3	0	3	6	9	12	15	18	21	24	27	30
4	0	4	8	12	16	20	24	28	32	36	40
5	0	5	10	15	20	25	30	35	40	45	50
6	0	6	12	18	24	30	36	42	48	54	60
7	0	7	14	21	28	35	42	49	56	63	70
8	0	8	16	24	32	40	48	56	64	72	80
9	0	9	18	27	36	45	54	63	72	81	90
10	0	10	20	30	40	50	60	70	80	90	100